Welcome to "Dining Secrets of Indiana"

If you are looking for a change of pace from the usual dining choices, then you will thoroughly enjoy the variety of opportunities right here at your fingertips! As you glance through the book, you won't find the familiar big city restaurants, chains and franchises. What you will find is an interesting journey through the small towns, back roads and suburbs of Indiana to some of the best-kept dining secrets in the state.

Content

Based on recommendations we received through a survey, we have published a wonderful collection of unique and memorable dining establishments, from small town, family owned businesses passed down through generations to several interesting historical landmarks; from very casual to formal and sophisticated decors; and from exotic European cuisines and ethnic foods to just good old American home-cookin'!

Through our research and owner input, we have made every effort to insure that the information about each restaurant is correct; however, please be aware that changes do occur.

Criteria for Selection

The restaurants that appear in "DINING SECRETS" *of* INDIANA" were not charged a fee to be included. Of the literally thousands of restaurants in Indiana, we personally selected those that we felt met our criteria for "uniqueness", whether it be food, history, people, decor, location, atmosphere, or some combination thereof.

Easy To Use

The book is arranged so you will find it convenient to use as you travel around the state.

- The state is broken down into 3 sections--Central, Northern & Southern Indiana.

- To identify the general location of a particular restaurant, open to the map on the inside front cover. The numbers next to each restaurant correspond with the numbers on the locator map.

- The cities and towns are listed alphabetically under each area in the index. When you're traveling through a particular area, check to see what restaurant is close by.

- Each restaurant lists an address, phone number, meals served and days open and closed to assist you in planning your visit.

- The book is designed to fit in a purse or glove compartment of the car so that it is readily available when you need it.

Enjoy!

As you travel around the state and have the opportunity to visit some of these wonderful eateries, we know you will enjoy the food and appreciate the charm and history behind so many of these one-of-a-kind establishments.

Please call us with any comments you have about this publication.

POOLE PUBLISHING
(800) 401-4599; (317) 849-9199

Central Indiana

Northern Indiana

Northern Indiana

Southern Indiana

Central Indiana

1. FLETCHER'S OF ATLANTA
185 W. Main, Atlanta, IN 46031
(765) 292-2777
Open Tuesday-Saturday for dinner only.

This peaceful, small town restaurant is just a short drive from Indianapolis and certainly worth the trip. One person said the following about Fletcher's: "Great fresh seafood in the midst of the cornfields. When available, the sea bass is as good as you'll find this side of Coronado Island."

2. BOGGSTOWN INN

6895 W. Boggstown Road, Boggstown, IN 46110
(317) 835-2020
Open Wednesday-Saturday for dinner by reservation only.

People from all 50 states and many foreign countries have made the trip to this small Indiana town for a nostalgic dose of ragtime music. Performers include duo piano, banjo, a small band, or singers (a different combination is offered each evening). Dinner is served by waitresses dressed in roaring '20's flapper attire and includes a choice of five entrees--prime rib, chicken, shrimp, a barbecued pork sandwich or a vegeterian platter, plus all the fixings. Cocktails and desserts are also available. Reservations are a must and should be made well in advance.

3. TOP NOTCH BAR & GRILL
113 South 3rd Street, Brookston, IN 47923
(765) 563-6508
Open Monday-Thursday for lunch & dinner; steak dinners only on Friday & Saturday.

Come with a big appetite on Friday and Saturday nights for excellent steaks, including the best filet mignon you will ever eat at a price you can't beat! Also, be prepared to share a good joke with Bob, the bartender, who is a walking joke book and is guaranteed to entertain you. "The long lines are worth the wait"...all in a casual and friendly atmosphere.

4. CHEZ JEAN
8821 South SR 67, Camby, IN 46113
(317) 831-0870
Open Tuesday-Friday for lunch & dinner; Saturday for dinner only.

Carl Huckaby, the 1996 American Culinary Federation's National Chef of the Year, has recently taken over this wonderful French restaurant where you can continue to enjoy its intimate and romantic atmosphere. Dining is available in 3 different settings: the handsome country room, the open and airy garden room, or the more formal French Provincial dining room, each offering authentic French cuisine with a Continental special on both the lunch and dinner menus. Dinner includes soup, salad, sorbet, entree, starch, vegetable and ala carte desserts, such as brulee, souffles, bourbon pecan pie or chocolate mousse. Lunch is less formal with an upscale American slant, featuring entrees such as chicken dijon, ground sirloin with hunter sauce, and veal bird.

5. ANVIL INN
29 East Jackson, Cicero, IN 46034
(317) 984-4533
Open Tuesday-Saturday for dinner only.
Closed Sunday & Monday.

The restaurant has evolved from a blacksmith shop in 1884 to a buggy shop, boat and motorcycle shop, and in 1974 the old building was gutted, a kitchen added, and restored again to look like a blacksmith shop! An additional room was later added to expand the dining area. The bar is decorated with an extensive miniature anvil collection and with other people's artifacts that are on loan. To maintain quality, the menu is limited to six steaks, ham steak, catfish, trout and shrimp, plus the popular pork chop special that is available Tuesday through Thursday only.

6. MILLER'S FISH SUPPERS

Box 173, Colfax, IN 46035
(765) 324-2656
Open Tuesday-Saturday
for dinner.

The small town atmosphere of downtown Colfax adds to the charm of this rustic-style restaurant whose reputation for "the best catfish and onion rings you will ever eat" draws customers from all over the surrounding area. Opened in 1946 as a family-owned business, the friendly staff offers over 230 years of combined experience. Meals are served family-style using only the finest ingredients, and a new, expanded menu offers more choices than ever before. In addition to their famous catfish, you can also enjoy tasty ribeye and T-bone steaks, broasted chicken, lobster, shrimp and scallops, plus baked potatoes are a recent addition.

7. BEEF HOUSE

I-74 & SR 63, 3 miles west of Covington, IN 47932
(765) 793-3947
Open Monday-Friday for breakfast, lunch
and dinner; dinner only on Saturday;
lunch and dinner on Sunday.

The Wright family purchased a small restaurant in 1963 and became well-known for their homemade rolls, a recipe secured at Purdue University while majoring in hotel/restaurant management. Today, they continue to be famous for the fact that all of the food served is "homemade", including wonderful soups and delicious pies. Plus, if you're in the mood for a terrific steak, this is the place to go!

8. MAPLE CORNER

1126 Liberty Street
Covington, IN 47932
(765) 793-2224

Open for dinner 7 evenings and lunch on Sunday.

This original 1931 roadhouse has been beautifully restored by the present owners and features several different dining rooms, each with its own unique atmosphere. Tiffany style windows and lamps add to the homey yet elegant surroundings, as do a variety of antiques and collectibles. Unique to Maple Corner is the use of sassafras and other native Indiana woods over a woodburning fire for grilling choice steaks and fresh seafood. They also feature an award-winning 1 lb. pork chop. The menu reflects the Midwestern tradition of "made from scratch", using locally grown fruits and vegetables. Homemade salad dressings, freshly baked breads, and seasonal desserts are a specialty. An in-house bakery also features all homemade items.

9. MAYBERRY CAFE

78 West Main Street, Danville, IN 46122
(317) 745-4067
Open daily for lunch & dinner.

If you're a fan of the Andy Griffith Show--as the owner obviously is!--you will appreciate the many pictures and other memorabilia that decorate the interior of this small town restaurant, appropriately named as well. The cafe-type decor includes lace tablecloths, brass chandeliers and an Aunt Bee's parlor atmosphere. A little of the big city charm is noticeable in the 40-50 item menu offering filets, orange roughy, prime rib, fried chicken and catfish. Make sure you save room for a piece of Aunt Bee's apple pie!

10. WOLFF'S TAVERN

1447 South A Street, Elwood, IN 46036
(765) 552-9022
Open Monday-Saturday for lunch & dinner;
closed Sunday.

This small town tavern is located in a century-old building with tin ceilings from the local tin factory, an old wooden bar, and paintings and beer signs covering the walls. The menu hasn't changed since the tavern opened, but customers continue to come to Wolff's for the roast beef Manhattans--they make their own gravy!--and breaded tenderloins, plus homemade potato and chili vegetable soups. Popular lunch specials include beef & noodles, cube steak, and fish. Before you leave, you must sample a piece of their homemade peanut butter, butterscotch or coconut cream pie!

11. EUGENE COVERED BRIDGE RESTAURANT

5787 N. Main Street, Eugene, IN 47928
(765) 492-7376
Open for lunch & dinner daily; breakfast on
Saturday & Sunday.

Located on the Big Vermillion River, you can look
out the back windows of the restaurant and view the
second longest single span covered bridge in
Indiana. Originally a grocery store and gas station
before extensive renovations, it now has the atmosphere of an old country store with framed historical
photos covering the walls, mementos of the town
history, and license plates from all 50 states plus
Canada, Venezuela and Argentina. The menu is
simply "good ol' Indiana food" served family style;
in fact, over 200 pounds of catfish are served each
week! On the weekends in spring, summer and fall,
you can order your choice of 22 homemade pies--
coconut cream is a favorite! (No alcohol served.)

12. HEISKELL'S

398 S. Main Street, Franklin, IN 46131
(317) 736-4900
Open Wednesday-Friday for lunch & dinner;
dinner only on Saturday; Sunday brunch.

You will enjoy dining in this turn-of-the-century
Victorian Manor House where all of the original
rooms are now used as dining rooms. Woodburning
fireplaces and leaded and stained glass accents add
to the charming atmosphere. The menu is basically
American cuisine--fresh seafood, chicken and beef
entrees. An extensive wine list and full bar are also
available, plus live entertainment on the grand
piano Friday and Saturday evenings.

13. ALMOST HOME

17 W. Franklin Street, Greencastle, IN 46135
(765) 653-5788
Open Monday-Saturday for lunch;
Thursday & Friday for dinner.

Window boxes filled with wildflowers decorate the
entrance to this unique tea room and gift shop,
specializing in delicious homemade soups, crois-
sant sandwiches, salads and delectable desserts. A
nice selection of specialty coffees and teas is also
available. After lunch, you will enjoy browsing in

the gift shop, featuring handcrafted gifts, home
decor items, Yankee candles and Davidson teas.
Surrounded by friendly people and many gift
items in a bright and cheerful setting, you feel as if
you're "almost home!"

14. DIFFERENT DRUMMER
The Walden Inn

2 Seminary Square, Greencastle, IN 46135
(765) 653-2761
Open daily for lunch & dinner (closed in between).

Best known for its integrity of service and upscale
cuisine, the restaurant in this quaint country inn
draws diners from all over the state. You will enjoy
a variety of outstanding entrees and equally
appealing appetizers and desserts prepared with
a regional flair, reflecting a touch of the chef's
classical continental background. A full service bar
and wine list offers a choice of refreshments to
accompany your meal. The Inn is open all year
'round except on Christmas Day.

15. COUNTRY COOK INN

10531 E. 180 S, Greentown, IN 46936
(765) 628-7676
Open Tuesday-Friday for lunch;
Tuesday-Saturday for dinner by reservation.

Located in a peaceful wooded setting on the
grounds of the owners' farm, this restaurant is a
unique energy-efficient structure incorporating the
simple concepts of earth-sheltered construction
and passive solar heating. The evening dinner
menu features popular specials each night, offering
portions that cater to both the hearty and the lighter
appetite. Their personal touch is also apparent in
the wide variety of items available for special health
needs, such as "low salt" substitute, dietetic ice
cream and low calorie salad dressings. Dinner by
reservation only.

16. CASA MIGUEL'S

102 South Madison, Greenwood, IN 46142
(317) 888-9010
Open Monday-Saturday for lunch and dinner;
closed Sunday.

A desire to go into the restaurant business, combined with an appreciation for Mexican food acquired through many trips to Mexico, led the owners to open Casa Miguel's 9 years ago. The original cook, whose roots were in Mexico, had a talent for preparing tasty, authentic dishes made from scratch, using fresh ingredients and no preservatives. The chili con queso and "chimi-chi-huahuas" (miniature chimichangas) are his special creations. Floutas, served with a pleasingly spicy sauce, are popular for lunch. The dinner menu offers everything from tacos to fajitas, the house specialty prepared with a choice of pork, steak or marinated chicken. Desserts include their famous hojulas (sugar cookies), served with your coffee.

17. JOHNSON COUNTY LINE RESTAURANT

1265 N. Madison Avenue, Greenwood, IN 46142
(317) 887-0404
Open daily for dinner.

Don't let the location in a strip center deceive you. Surrounded by wood from old Johnson County barns, hardwood floors, and candlelight on the tables, you will enjoy dining in this quiet, relaxed atmosphere. Murals on the walls were painted by a Butler University friend, depicting scenes of the California wine country. Between 75 and 150 wines are available at all times, and 4 course gourmet-style wine tasting parties are offered in this unique setting. The regular menu includes prime rib, hand-cut steaks, beef kabobs, seafood and poultry dishes, plus there is always a vegetarian main course.

18. WELLIVERS

On State Road 38, Hagerstown, IN 47346
(765) 489-4131
Open Thursday-Saturday evenings for dinner;
lunch and dinner on Sunday.

In 1947, Guy Welliver bought a restaurant in Hagerstown that seated 50 people. Today, there is a seating capacity of 500! The buffet that features steamed shrimp and pan-fried chicken has made them famous throughout the area. You can order from the menu or treat yourself to one of the blackboard specials. Some also recommend that you select one of the booths in the bar.

19. BAZBEAUX PIZZA

334 Massachusetts Ave.
Indianapolis, IN 46204
(317) 636-7662
Open Monday-Saturday for lunch & dinner; dinner only on Sunday.

Bazbeaux was the whimsical name given to a court jester, whose cleverness was used to create new dishes to amuse the courts he served. In 1986, the Bazbeaux legend was brought to Indianapolis as the first restaurant in the area to introduce pizza lovers to a new concept: unique combinations of sometimes exotic toppings on a choice of whole wheat or white crust. Building on the success of the Broad Ripple location, they expanded to this old store building in "downtown's art and threatre district." Lunch specials include pizza by the slice. Pizza alla quattro formaggio is the most popular--5 cheeses, bacon and mushrooms. The muffaletta and stromboli sandwiches are also in demand. Beer, wine and espresso are available. While you're there, look for the mural of Bazbeaux serving pizza to the king!

20. DEETER & GABE'S

1462 West 86th Street, Indianapolis, IN 46260
(317) 876-1111   (North Willow Commons)
Open Monday-Saturday for lunch & dinner;
dinner only on Sunday.

With a new concept in mind, Dieter, the successful chef/owner of the Glass Chimney, joined with his maitre d', Gabriel, and opened a neighborhood restaurant with a warm, casual atmosphere where local people like to gather. The menu specializes in rotisserie and wood-fired oven entrees prepared in the open kitchen with wonderfully unique and attractively presented specials offered each day. Pork loin is a favorite item, served with a choice of 8 different sauces. Fresh seafood is also featured daily, as well as five different soups--"the veal soup is both hearty and wonderful." The same menu is available for both lunch and dinner with your choice of regular or large portions. The entrees are truly a taste treat!

21. G.T. SOUTH'S RIB HOUSE

5711 East 71st Street, Indianapolis, IN 46220
(317) 849-6997
Open Monday-Saturday for lunch & dinner;
closed Sunday.

As you enter G.T. South's Rib House, the aroma of smoked BBQ fills the air and whets the appetite. The owner hails from the south and wanted to bring authentic barbecue to Indianapolis. He claims that barbecue chefs argue about whose barbecue is the best, but they all agree: "Cook it low and smoke it slow." The pulled pork sandwich with hot or mild sauce, served with coleslaw and chips, is clearly the most popular item, but smoked turkey and beef brisket are also available. For larger appetites, the baby back ribs ("wet" or "dry"), rib tips, and platters are truly satisfying. A full-service bar with big screen TV and a player piano provide entertainment in a very casual and relaxed setting.

22. HOLLYHOCK HILL

8110 North College Ave., Indianapolis, IN 46240
(317) 251-2294
Open Tuesday-Saturday for dinner; Sunday for lunch & dinner; closed Monday.

In 1928, the original owners began serving dinners at their Country Cottage in Northern Marion County. Because of the many beautiful hollyhocks on the premises, it soon became known as Hollyhock Hill. One of a few family-style restaurants still in existence in the U.S., Hollyhock stands out from others not only for the excellent food but for its more formal ambience created by floral curtains and fresh flowers on the tables in each of the light and airy dining rooms. Steaks and shrimp are on the menu, but the fried chicken "like mother used to make" is the most popular, accompanied by a feast of vegetables, salad with their famous sweet-sour dressing, homemade pickled beets, apple butter and

hot baked bread. Ice cream with a choice of toppings to make your own sundae completes this memorable dining experience.

23. IARIA'S ITALIAN RESTAURANT

317 S. College Avenue, Indianapolis, IN 46202
(317) 638-7706
Open Tuesday-Friday for lunch & dinner; dinner only on Saturday; closed Sunday & Monday.

The Iaria family came to the United States from Calabria, located at the very tip of the boot of Italy. This family-owned restaurant opened in 1936 and continues to offer wonderful Italian dishes prepared from recipes that have passed down through generations. Very little has changed over the years from the original decor, but the comfortable atmosphere makes it an inviting place to bring the family. The lunch and dinner menus are the same, offering meat and spinach ravioli, homemade meatballs and Italian sausage, pastas served with your choice of homemade sauces, plus delicious homemade garlic bread. You'll also enjoy the cheesecake, cannoli, or spumoni for dessert.

24. KABUL RESTAURANT

8553 Ditch Road, Indianapolis, Indiana 46260
(Greenbriar Shopping Center)
(317) 257-1213
Open Monday-Saturday for dinner only.

"A taste so different from 99% of Indy's restaurants", as one customer stated, is why the owner wanted to offer the Indianapolis community a taste of cuisines from his country of Afghanistan. A mural of Bala Hissar, a 6th century military fort in Kabul, commands your attention, whether eating in the main dining room or on the upper deck. The food is prepared in an immaculate kitchen where no chemicals or preservatives are used. Afghan bread dipped in a special chutney is a tasty companion to the Aush (special noodle) soup. Steamed dumplings filled with leeks or ground beef and topped with yogurt can be eaten alone or accompanied by beef, lamb, or cornish hen. Seasoned brown rice with carrot strips, raisins and almonds also complement the entrees. Interesting dessert choices include "firnee" (milk pudding topped with pistachios), "jelabi" (coils of pastry) and "baklava" (sweet layers of filo, honey and nuts.)... "Delicious!"

ንግስት ሳባ ም⁹ብ ቤት

25. QUEEN OF SHEBA
936 Indiana Avenue, Indianapolis, IN 46202
(317) 638-8426
Open Tuesday-Friday for lunch & dinner;
Saturday for dinner; Sunday for groups of 10 or
more; closed Monday.

Your hostess, Abeba (Aby), came to Indianapolis to go to school but decided to open this Ethiopian restaurant instead! As stated on the menu, "prepare yourself for an unforgettable dining experience." As you enter the colorful restaurant, you immediately realize you are being exposed to another culture. The tables feature low cushioned chairs that are placed around a "Messob", a hand-sewn circular grass vessel. According to Ethiopian custom, gathering to eat, sharing the same plate and the bread called "Injera" creates a bond of friendship and personal loyalty. The crepe-like Injera is used to pick up bites of food from the round serving tray, filled with stews, beef dishes, a variety of vegetables, and herb and tangy sauces, all prepared from natural ingredients. Spiced Ethiopian tea and coffee are available, along with beer and wine.

26. SNAX
2413 East 65th Street, Indianapolis, IN 46220
(317) 257-6291
Open Monday-Saturday for dinner & late snacks.

This is the place to go if you're looking for just a bite to eat rather than a full meal, or a late snack after other restaurants are closed! Owned by the same proprietor of "Something Different", a well-known gourmet restaurant, Snax is located next door and was designed to be a "grazing" restaurant. A stack of plates in the center of the table invite you to help yourself to 18 different appetizers that change with the seasons. You can also enjoy your choice of 26 single malt scotches along with seasonal beers, some from small breweries.

27. THREE SISTERS CAFE & BAKERY
6360 N. Guilford Avenue, Indianapolis, IN 46220
(317) 257-5556
Open Tuesday-Sunday for breakfast, lunch &
dinner; closed Monday.

The name of this interesting establishment and the food served embodies a Native American concept that is hundreds of years old: "Food is sacred and enjoyment of it with friends is a gift." The mostly vegetarian menu honors the belief that these gifts come to us from nature. The "three sisters" are corn, beans and squash: the corn and beans are planted together in a mound and the corn stalk provides a trellis for the winding bean plant; the squash, with its large leaves, is planted in between to fight off the weeds and help maintain moisture in the soil. With these ingredients in mind, try the "Three Sisters Casserole" for dinner! The menu also features chicken, turkey and salmon entrees, breakfast eggs with numerous vegetable combinations, a delightful assortment of soups, sandwiches and salads, plus the powerhouse potatoes are a must. The owners have maintained the integrity of this old house and have a dozen tables available, some looking out over the herb garden. Both beer and wine are also available.

28. MEL'S DINER
132 East Main Street, Knightstown, IN 46148
(765) 345-7688
Open Monday-Saturday for lunch & dinner.

A father-daughter team opened this restaurant in space that was formerly a hardware and grocery store, and the kitchen was originally a carriage house. Poplar wood from an old sawmill covers the walls that are decorated with towel racks, complete with terry cloth towels, mirrors and brass accents. Blue grass musicians come to eat and play on Monday and Friday. Customers can select one of several entrees that are available each day, such as pork barbecue, fettucini alfredo or beef Manhattan on Monday and pan fried chicken or ham & bean soup with hoecakes on Saturday. Enjoy one of their homemade pies for dessert. (No alcohol served.)

29. PATOUT'S OF NEW ORLEANS

3614 State Road 38 East, Lafayette, IN 47905
(765) 447-5400
Open daily for lunch & dinner.

Now in its third generation of family ownership, Patout's originally opened in 1913 in New Iberia, Louisiana, the home of Tabasco sauce. With a mural of Preservation Hall on the wall, a picket fence from a New Orleans plantation, and authentic Cajun music piped in daily, you'll feel like you're dining on Bourbon Street! A live jazz trio plays on Friday and Saturday nights and Sunday lunch. The food is also authentic Cajun, a collection of family recipes featuring shrimp creole, red beans and rice, Jambalaya, and gumbo with seafood flown in fresh from Louisiana. Note--there's Yankee food, too!

30. SARGE OAK'S

721 Main Street, Lafayette, IN 47901
(765) 742-5230
Open Tuesday-Friday for lunch & dinner; dinner only on Saturday; closed Sunday & Monday.

Established over 60 years ago, Sarge Oak's continues to be one of Indiana's "Hidden Treasures"! The game parlor setting of the '30's and '40's has been recreated in the dining room with an atmosphere reminiscent of that era. Early period hanging lights, Sarge's hunting trophy, and early 1900 hand-colored photographs by Wallace Nutting decorate the interior. Call early and request the "Cooler", a cozy little booth that seats 4-6 people. (Everyone thought this only held the beer and steaks!)They are famous for their aged fresh cut steaks, daily seafood and poultry specials, plus the french fries are made daily, never frozen.

31. SNOW BEAR FROZEN CUSTARD

Near Columbia Park, Lafayette, IN 47902
Open daily for lunch & dinner in summer;
hours vary off season.

"I can't resist recommending the frozen custard at the corner of Main Street and Wallace Avenue. The menu is very casual, featuring a choice of sandwiches and hot dogs, but dessert is their specialty! None can compare..." You must stop by when you are in the vicinity to enjoy the best banana split you have ever tasted!

32. HEARTHSTONE RESTAURANT

18149 U.S. 52, Metamora, IN 47030
(765) 647-5204
Open Tuesday-Sunday for lunch & dinner.
Closed Monday. Winter hours vary.

Located in a quaint little town with over 100 craft shops, a grist mill, riverboat and railroad, the Hearthstone is a well-known landmark at the edge of town. Casual dining is offered in a country atmosphere--you can relax on the porch overlooking the canal, or enjoy your meal inside by the huge stone fireplace. Popular menu items served all day include pan-fried chicken, country cured ham, catfish, and charbroiled steaks. Everything is made from scratch, including wonderful biscuits and homemade pies. Recognized in Midwest Living magazine.

33. KOPPER KETTLE

US Route 52, Morristown, IN 46161
(765) 763-6767
Open Tuesday-Sunday for lunch & dinner.

In business since 1923, the Kopper Kettle has a delightfully restful atmosphere where you can savor their famous Hoosier fried chicken, broiled prime steaks and delicious seafood, served family-style. The large quaint house is a veritable art museum, displaying a fascinating collection of art objects from many parts of the world. From the beautiful antique furnishings and artifacts to the balconies, fountains and strolling gardens, the Kopper Kettle has a distinctive charm unmatched by the finest European restaurants.

34. FOXFIRES

3300 Chadam Lane, Muncie, IN 47304
(765) 284-5235
Open Monday-Saturday for dinner only.

Owned since 1984 by Jim Davis of "Garfield" fame, there is both a formal and casual restaurant under one roof. The decor is very warm and contemporary with local artwork displayed on the walls. The extensive wine collection includes a 10,000 bottle wine cellar in the main dining room and a twelve-bottle cruvinet in the casual, open bar area. Chef specialties include wild game and fresh seafood delivered 3 times per week, but unique and in demand is Portland, Indiana ostrich. Customers find this low-fat, low-cholesterol entree a tasty alternative to beef!

35. CLASSIC KITCHEN

610 Hannibal Street, Noblesville, IN 46060
(317) 773-7385
Open Tuesday-Saturday for lunch; Friday and Saturday for dinner. Reservations requested.

Located just south of the Noblesville courthouse, this marvelous restaurant offers fine dining in a light and airy French-style setting. Gourmet magazine calls the fare "eclectic geographic food" which is a reflection of the extensive travels of the chef/proprietor. All entrees are prepared "in house" with quality, healthy products--no additives or preservatives are used. The lunch menu features homemade soups, quiche, whole wheat crepes, and their own natural ice creams with vanilla shortbreads. Tea is served after lunch from 2-4 pm. Candlelight dinners on Friday and Saturday nights include classic specialties of veal, chicken, fish and vegetables, plus a changing repertoire of French and Belgian chocolate desserts.

36. PENDLETON HOUSE

118 N. Pendleton Avenue, Pendleton, IN 46064
(765) 778-8061
Open Monday-Saturday for lunch; dinner only on Friday & Saturday; closed Sunday.

Enjoy "afternoon tea" (Monday-Friday, 2:30-4 pm) on the large porch or garden room in this uniquely decorated Victorian home. Lunch is served daily in the downstairs dining rooms; candlelight dinners are served on Friday and Saturday nights in the private rooms upstairs. Once a month in the Fall, a "Shaker Night" dinner is served with plenty of good home cooked dishes. Call or stop by and sign the guest book to receive a monthly schedule.

37. GRANT STREET BAR & GRILL

26 North Grant Street, Peru, IN 46970
(765) 472-3997
Open Monday-Friday for lunch;
Tuesday-Saturday for dinner; closed Sunday.

The location may be remembered as Froggie's Log Cabin, but today you will find fine dining in a casual atmosphere--no ties are expected! Trained at the Culinary Institute of America, the chef has returned to his roots in Indiana and enjoys the challenge of subtly presenting new ingredients into traditional dishes that Hoosiers like to eat. Thus, the menu features the standard entrees but they are embellished with tasty surprises, such as a seared filet of beef with brandy mushroom cream sauce, or chicken breast stuffed with spinach and feta cheese. You'll enjoy this change from the ordinary!

38. SIDING BY THE TRACKS

8 West 10th Street (Downtown), Peru, IN 46970
(765) 473-4041
Open Tuesday-Friday for lunch & dinner;
dinner only on Saturday; Sunday brunch.

Train buffs will love dining in one of two restored railroad cars or in a dining room embellished with antiques and train memorabilia. In fact, the owner calls himself a "railroad junkie"! Both a lunch buffet and smaller dinner buffet are available or you can order off the menu, except on Friday when diners come to feast on the popular seafood buffet. Black Diamond steak is a house specialty, and outstanding desserts include Kahlua ice cream pie and homemade cheesecakes.

39. OLDE RICHMOND INN

138 South Fifth Street, Richmond, IN 47374
(765) 962-2247
Open daily for lunch & dinner.

Located in the old Richmond area, this former 1892 residence exhibits the work of local "south-end Dutch" wood craftsmen and masons. The Victorian setting is accented with Italian decorative tiles, a stained glass wall from the 1800's, and custom stained glass fixtures designed by Richmond and Cincinnati craftsmen. A unique chandelier from the home of Micajah Henley, the inventor of roller skates, lights the north dining room and three fireplaces add to the warm and inviting atmosphere. Special meals are prepared daily and served in a gracious and professional manner. To whet the appetite, sample the shrimp bianca appetizer, a house specialty. The American and continental-style menu offers a wonderful variety of prime cut steaks and chops, seafood, chicken and pasta entrees for dinner, salad plates, sandwich platters, and chef's casserole of the day for lunch, plus many daily blackboard specials.

40. RED ONION
406 South Main, Sheridan, IN 46069
(317) 758-0424
Open Tuesday-Saturday evenings for dinner;
closed Sunday & Monday.

This small town restaurant on Main Street was purchased by the present owners in 1992. They pride themselves on great food served in a comfortable, casual atmosphere that draws patrons from all over Central Indiana. In fact, about 95% of their customers are from out of town. They are best known for the breaded tenderloin, hand-cut daily and

served on a 7" round bun, but those who have eaten there believe it's a 10" bun! All of the sandwiches are large and cater to a hearty appetite, but feel free to split one with a friend. Popular dinner items include hand-cut steaks, catfish and prime rib.

41. STOOKEY'S
125 East Main Street, Thorntown, IN 46071
(765) 436-7202
Open Tuesday-Saturday for dinner.

If you're in the mood for some great catfish or a tasty ribeye steak, plus "out-of-this-world" onion rings, then head to Stookey's. Open for business since 1975, the entire Stookey family is still involved in the operation of the restaurant and dedicated to upholding its fine reputation. Race fans will appreciate the "500" decor in the bar.

42. IVANHOES
398 S. Main Street, Upland, IN 46989
(765) 998-7261
Open daily for lunch & dinner.

If you have a craving for delicious ice cream, you must stop at Ivanhoe's but you might have a tough time choosing from the more than 100 different varieties available! Good old-fashioned hamburgers plus excellent salads are another reason to stop here. Ivanhoes started as a drive-in in the '60s and has grown into a large, popular place to eat. Forget the diet and watching the fat grams because this is worth it!

43. GISELA'S KAFFEEKRANZCHEN
112 South Main Street, Zionsville, IN 46077
(317) 873-5523
Open Tuesday-Saturday for lunch & dinner;
Sunday brunch; closed on Monday.

Guests climb a narrow staircase to this second floor restaurant that is truly in the rafters! Gisela, the restaurant's namesake, was homesick for her German culture so she filled the space with mementos of life in Germany: books, posters, flags, china, mugs and bottles decorate the interior. A European atmosphere is created by high ceilings, brick walls, huge windows covered with lace curtains and flowers on the tables. The dinner menu features Korelette Tirol (pork chops), filet goulash-stroganoff, schweinbraten (pork roast), rinds rouladen, weinerschnitzel, and sauerbraten, served· with German potatoes, red cabbage and green beans. The lunch and brunch menus vary, and there is a nice assortment of beers and wines available. If you have a taste for authentic German food, then this is definitely a place you will enjoy.

44. PANACHE
60 South Elm Street, Zionsville, IN 46077
(317) 873-1388
Open Tuesday-Saturday for lunch & dinner; closed Sunday & Monday.

Since the age of 14, proprietor Richard Cottance has worked in various European and North African restaurants. He learned through these experiences that in the family-owned European bistro, food is professionally and innovatively presented without having to deal with the "stuffed shirts". When Panache opened in June, 1992, the intent was to dispel the myth that fine food and wine required "diamonds and gold", and the owner has accomplished just that. Panache provides the best of fine dining in the comfortable setting of a small old house where you dine in the quaint and cozy rooms. The kitchen is small and the menu is short, but chef Michael David enjoys creating an eclectic mix of wonderful contemporary American dishes. Five entrees are available each day, featuring fish, meat, poultry and always a vegetarian choice. An enticing example is the sauteed veal strips with Mediterranean vegetables, served on a bed of pasta with gorgonzola cream sauce.

Northern Indiana

45. CAPTAIN'S CABIN SUPPER CLUB
3070 West Shadyside Road, Angola, IN 46703
(219) 665-5663
Open for dinner Monday-Saturday in Summer; Wednesday-Saturday in Winter.

Built in the late 1800's, there is quite a history surrounding this old log cabin that is now a fine dining establishment. Originally a trading post, boarding house, ice house, and fish house, it served as a convenient stop for early settlers and travelers. Today, you can relax and enjoy a superb lobster, seafood or choice steak dinner as you reflect on those earlier times in history.

46. THE HATCHERY
118 South Elizabeth Street, Angola, IN 46703
(219) 665-9957
Open Monday-Saturday for dinner only.

The name of this restaurant originated from the fact that the building was actually a chicken hatchery in the early 1900's. Now you can enjoy fine dining in an intimate, formal setting, accented with midnight blue and pink colors, dim lighting, flowers, candles, and a baby grand piano. The Hatchery specializes in fresh seafood flown in daily from a fishing fleet in Florida and a fresh seafood menu is printed daily. Steak and lamb are also offered. Your favorite wine can be ordered off their extensive wine list, recognized by Wine Spectator's Award of Excellence since 1991.

47. DUTCH MILL RESTAURANT
402 North Main Street, Bluffton, IN 46714
(219) 824-4000
Open Monday-Friday for breakfast, lunch & dinner; Saturday for breakfast & lunch; closed Sunday.

Since 1948 when Glen Moser purchased the Dutch Mill, it has taken root along the banks of the Wabash and flowered. From its early days of having only three booths and a dozen counter seats, it now offers "a good variety of good food" in 12 different dining rooms. The homemade pies are obviously popular--the oven can bake 36 pies at one time! The homemade bread and rolls are also a treat.

48. PINDER'S
South Main & Ohio Streets, Culver, IN 46511
(219) 842-3415
Open Tuesday-Saturday for dinner; Sunday 11-3 (winter), 11-8 (resort season). Closed January & February.

A family-owned and operated restaurant spanning 4 generations, the owners take pride in the fact that all of the family works there regularly. Near Lake Maxinkuckee, the building was originally a bait house. A window sandwich shop was eventually added, followed by indoor seating. Family memorabilia and paintings by local friends add color to the southwestern decor of the dining area that now seats 170. Their reputation for good home-cooked meals draws customers who enjoy the daily specials of meatloaf, chicken fried steak, and creamed chicken & biscuits, or steaks, chops and seafood from the regular menu. A full soup and salad bar with homemade dressings is one daughter's specialty; a daughter-in-law makes the cakes and the "very best" sugar cookies. Homemade pies are also available on the weekends. A delicious buffet is offered on Friday, Saturday and Sunday.

49. BACK FORTY JUNCTION
1011 North 13th Street, Decatur, IN 46733
(219) 724-3355
Open for lunch and dinner daily.

This establishment opened in the early 1950's and is "one big antique, from one end to the other," according to the manager. A caboose car sits outside and Tiffany lamps, as well as a lamp from Carole Lombard's home, light the interior. The fare here is "good home cooking" served smorgasbord style and includes fresh-baked bread.

50. MATTERHORN
2041 Cassopolis Street, Elkhart, IN 46514
(219) 262-1500
Open Monday-Friday for lunch & dinner; dinner only on Saturday; Sunday brunch.

Once a small, casual dining spot in a chalet-type building, this restaurant now features fine dining in an elegant atmosphere, embellished with dark blue carpet, gold-tone walls and heavy brass light fixtures. A vaulted ceiling with natural beams and decorative accents, including stained glass and Impressionist prints covering the walls, also add to the formal ambience. The menu offers a wonderful selection of entrees featuring lamb, veal, excellent steaks and fresh seafood, including salmon, sole and walleye. A seafood buffet is available on Fridays. To complement the lunch buffet, one of 30 different and tasty soup recipes from the chef's collection is offered as the daily special.

51. CAFE JOHNELL

2529 S. Calhoun
Fort Wayne, IN 46807
(219) 456-1939
Open Monday-Saturday for dinner (Monday variable); closed Sunday.

This distinctive 4-star restaurant offers fine dining in an elegant atmosphere, enhanced by the extensive art collection decorating the interior. The French cuisine includes a wonderful selection of appetizers, soups, salads and entrees prepared from the highest quality food possible, with fresh fish from Boston, prime aged beef from Iowa, and veal from Wisconsin. For that special occasion, romantic dinners for two include Chateaubriand and Filet De Boeuf Wellington. A choice of wines from their outstanding wine cellar completes a memorable dining experience.

52. HARTLEY'S
4301 S. Fairfield Ave., Fort Wayne, IN 46807
(219) 744-3141
Open Monday-Friday for lunch & dinner; dinner only on Saturday; closed Sunday.

Named after the restaurant's owners, Hartley, Sr. and Hartley, Jr. combined their experience in the restaurant business with a love for the area through their involvement with the Ft. Wayne Komets hockey team and opened this establishment in 1983. Dine by candlelight in a small, intimate setting, decorated with paintings by local artists on the walls. The continental cuisine offers the freshest food available, prepared on a mesquite or flat grill. Many selections are pan sauteed or broiled with very few deep fried items on the menu.

53. ITALIAN CONNECTION

2725 Taylor Street, Fort Wayne, IN 46802
(219) 432-9702
Open Wednesday-Saturday for dinner only.

This could be the best connection you will ever make if you're interested in handmade pastas, homemade Italian ice cream and thick, creamy cheesecake. Everything served is Italian, including a selection of fine wines and beers to enjoy with your meal. Take time to view all the quaint old family photos lining the walls.

54. SHOPOFF'S

12012 US 24 West, Fort Wayne, IN 46804
(219) 672-3952
Open Monday-Saturday for dinner only.

In a building described by the owner as "older than dirt", this neighborhood restaurant in a residential area has the classic "tavern down the street" feeling where customers just drop in and everybody knows each other. A set menu includes steaks, chicken and seafood, but a feature board highlights Bob Shopoff's own dishes, many based on his Macedonian heritage. He admits to being called the "soup god" and takes pride in concoctions that often rely on customers for their name: black bean, jalepeno chili with filet tips, cabbage/sauerkraut and pork are just a few examples!

55. BRICK HOUSE RESTAURANT

16820 County Road 38, Goshen, IN 46526
(219) 534-4949
Open Tuesday-Friday for lunch; dinner only on Saturday; closed Sunday & Monday.

This original 1870 house includes nine dining rooms on two floors, decorated in a Williamsburg theme with oil lamps on the tables, antique-style chairs, and family pictures on the walls. As you look around the interior, you are reminded of the charm and character of homes in that era by the unique molding, window panes, and a service bar that is the home's original china cabinet. The menu offers a continental cuisine with daily fresh catch, veal, and lobster entrees.

56. CHECKERBERRY INN

62644 County Road 37, Goshen, IN 46526
(219) 642-4445
Open for dinner Tuesday-Saturday from April to December; Friday & Saturday only in February and March.

Situated off a sparsely traveled road in the seclusion of Amish farmland, the Checkerberry is reminiscent of a gracious European Country Inn. Thirteen individually decorated rooms and suites offer breathtaking views of the unspoiled rolling countryside. The restaurant serves only the freshest foods available, using herbs and other ingredients from the local countryside. Fine wines are available to complement your meal.

57. PHIL SMIDT & SON

1205 North Calumet Avenue, Hammond, IN 46320
(219) 659-0025; (800) 376-4534
Open Monday-Saturday for lunch & dinner; dinner only on Sunday. (Closed Sundays January-April.)

From its humble beginnings as a 12-seat, 3 table dining room with a 12-foot bar and attached boat livery to its notoriety today as a world famous restaurant, Phil Smidt's continues to maintain its reputation for quality food and service that began in 1910. The frog legs served here have been celebrated for all of the 80+ years that the restaurant has been in business, along with the famous lake perch, served whole or boned and cooked to perfection. When you visit Phil Smidt's, be sure to ask to be seated in the Rose Room! Your dining experience won't be complete, however, without a piece of warm gooseberry pie.

58. FIFTH STREET DELI

431 Washington St. (corner of 5th & Washington)
Michigan City, IN 46360
(219) 872-5204
Open 7 days a week for lunch (lunch & dinner during summer).

Located in an old house just a block from Lighthouse Mall, the Deli serves sandwiches, soups, salads and desserts all day long. Enjoy the fifties atmosphere complete with popular music of that decade while dining on the main floor or upstairs. Sandwiches carry the names of popular actors and actresses from the era: Greta Garbo, Frank Sinatra, the Cisco Kid, Clark Gable, Rudy Valentino, etc. A favorite is the "Marilyn" sandwich, a chicken breast topped with Canadian bacon and covered with cheese on a garlic roll. Soups are made daily with "whatever sounds good"! Chicken salad with walnuts and similar salad plates are frequent requests. Desserts are wonderful and particularly tasty after a day of shopping!

59. MILLER BAKERY CAFE

555 S. Lake St., Miller Beach (Gary), IN 46403
(219) 938-2229
Open for lunch Tuesday-Friday;
dinner Tuesday-Sunday; closed Monday.

As you approach the landmark Miller Bakery, built in 1941, the old storefront is no indication of what you'll find inside! Open the door and you are treated to an exciting array of colors, from the wood floors to the creamy marble and cobalt blue walls. High ceilings with exposed duct work and tables covered with paper and crayons add to the atmosphere, along with some of the original pastry cabinets that are on display. Background music varies from Billie Holliday to New-Age on any given day. The lunch and dinner menus specialize in a global cuisine that changes with the seasons, featuring such items as fresh Thai salmon filet, midwestern pork chops, Indiana duck breast, sea scallops with corn, and shittake mushrooms.

60. BEAVER DAM

1200 North Francis, Monticello, IN 47960
(219) 583-8375
Open Wednesday-Saturday for dinner.

Enjoy the eclectic atmosphere and friendly small town staff in this family owned and operated establishment, featuring nouveau-style nightly specials. An extensive menu features unique pastas, grilled seafood, and slow roasted prime rib, accompanied by palate-pleasing homemade soups, hot baked French bread and garden greens. Complete your dining experience with one of their homemade pies or southern pecan bread pudding with hot bourbon sauce, or perhaps an after dinner cocktail. All special dietary requests are granted by their informed kitchen staff.

61. OAKDALE INN

Highway 39 & 421, Monticello, IN 47960
(219) 965-9104
Open Tuesday-Sunday for lunch & dinner;
closed Monday.

Enjoy great food and entertainment at this funky place in the country (between Delphi & Monticello) serving "the best catfish by a dam site", according to the owner. Located near Lake Freeman at the Oakdale Dam, this 1943 bait house and restaurant has grown over the years to now accommodate 140 people. The owner's sense of humor is quite apparent as you view the interesting gadgets and gags around the bar--a mongoose in a cage, a boot saver, etc.--and watch out for the hanging buckets that occasionally drop from the ceiling! Catfish, whole or fileted, is the house specialty, but the steaks are also "top-of-the-line." Pork filets are a popular lunch choice, and 8 different beers are available on tap. Entertainment on Friday and Saturday nights features a sing-along with Cawood Greene, plus a chance to tell your favorite jokes!

62. HANNAH'S

115 South Whittaker, New Buffalo, MI 49117
(616) 469-1440
Open daily for lunch & dinner except Christmas Day. Reservations welcome.

Hannah's is located just across the Indiana/ Michigan border (I-94, Exit #1) in the quaint little town of New Buffalo where you will find a variety of wonderful shops and unique boutiques. When you need a break from a day of shopping, this is the perfect place to stop for lunch or dinner. Formerly a home built in 1895, the owners have maintained a warm and friendly atmosphere and a genuine hospitality where you feel like a guest in their home. The decor is an eclectic collection of antiques and artifacts, and photos of family and friends dot the walls. The menu is one of the most extensive in the area, catering to everyone's tastes and featuring a nice selection of appetizers, entrees, sandwiches, salads, and vegetarian dishes. The full roasted prime rib and Bohemian roast duck and pork, served with dumplings and sauerkraut, are popular dinner choices.

63. HAYLOFT

15147 Lincolnway West, Plymouth, IN 46563
(219) 936-6680
Open Monday-Saturday for dinner; closed Sunday.

Dine in a turn-of-the-century barn that definitely has a personality of its own! The owners are antique buffs, which you will notice as you look around the interior. There are tales of a resident ghost named Homer, a farmer who died of a heart attack at the entrance to the barn. In fact, both employees and guests verify his existence. If you have the urge to try something different, sample the barbequed buffalo and alligator appetizers, or the ostrich filet entree. However, the more traditional fare is also available, including prime rib, smoked barbequed ribs, seafood and pasta dishes.

64. CITY OFFICE & PUB

114 S. Van Rensselaer St., Rensselaer, IN 47978
(219) 866-9916
Open Tuesday-Saturday for lunch & dinner;
lunch only on Monday; closed Sunday.

As the county seat, Rensselaer needed a convenient eating spot so the City Pub opened to fill that void. In the process of renovating the space that used to be a pharmacy, signs of the original design and decor were uncovered, including restaurant booths

and brick-tile inlaid archways. The antique atmosphere has been maintained, creating a comfortable setting for both locals and visitors. A collage of old courthouses and pictures of politicians decorate the walls. Additional seating is available at the 120-foot long bar or on the elevated porch. Steaks are the specialty, but prime rib, pan-fried lake perch, BBQ ribs and chicken wings are also popular choices.

65. SOLLY'S

Highway 24, Reynolds, IN 47980
(219) 984-5512
Open Tuesday-Saturday for dinner only;
closed Sunday & Monday.

The original owner of Solly's, Mr. Solomon, spent 42 years building "a steak house, pure and simple, no fancy adjectives." Even though he no longer owns the business, his traditions continue. The new owners are also committed to hand-cutting the meats, grinding their own hamburger, and tossing the salad with Solly's famous red arrow dressing. In keeping with the Southwestern decor, you will find a totem pole outside and 2 red arrows with an Indian head over the fireplace. Choice aged steaks are the house specialty, but broasted chicken and ocean catfish are also popular items.

66. AMBRIOLA'S RESTAURANTE

112 North Main Street, Roanoke, IN 46783
(219) 672-3097
Open Tuesday-Saturday for dinner;
closed Sunday & Monday.

Ambriola's was opened in 1984 by the Ambriole family and at least one family member is always present during business hours. Over 90% of the items on their menu are made on the premises, including wonderful pastas, sauces and desserts. The person who submitted this recommendation stated that "Ambriola's serves the best food in Huntington County."

67. ROANOKE VILLAGE INN

190 Main (Off US 24 West), Roanoke, IN 46783
(219) 672-3707
Open Monday-Saturday for lunch & dinner;
closed Sunday.

Simply "a bar with great food" is how this full
service bar and restaurant was described by a
Huntington resident. They are best known for both
the broiled and deep fried haddock and the popular
16 oz. barbecued pork chop. Additional choices
include barbecued ribs, a full line of steaks, and
chicken entrees.

68. TEIBEL'S RESTAURANT

U.S. 30 & 41, Schererville, IN 46375
(219) 865-2000
Open daily for lunch & dinner.

Teibel's first opened its doors in 1929 and has operated continuously ever since. Customers come here
for the delicious chicken and lake perch that have
made them famous throughout the area. In fact, the
family who submitted this recommendation said
they have yet to find any other place whose lake
perch can compare to Teibel's. Banquet facilities
are also available for business meetings or any
occasion--call for banquet menu information.

69. LASALLE GRILL

115 West Colfax Avenue, South Bend, IN 46601
(219) 288-1155, (800) 382-9323
Open Monday-Saturday for dinner only.
Closed Sundays, except Easter & Mother's Day.

LaSalle Grill has a well-deserved reputation for
providing guests with a unique and memorable
dining experience unlike any other in the area. Dine
in a lively, upscale casual atmosphere where you
can enjoy classic jazz piano on Friday and Saturday
evenings. A separate barroom and cigar salon
provide a relaxed setting both before and after your
meal. The cuisine is modern American--a blend of
many classic and ethnic ingredients using only
the highest quality and freshest foods available.
Items change daily to reflect the seasons and are

designed to stimulate and intrigue the palate; the
presentation is unique, creative, and tastefully
prepared. In addition to a superb selection of
appetizers, desserts, and an award-winning wine
list, there is an outstanding choice of entrees--rack
of New Zealand lamb, pan-crisped breast of
Indiana duckling, and their own dry aged prime top
sirloin steak, to name just a few. Noted for their
cigar dinners and wine tastings, these and other
specialty theme dinners are held frequently and
feature the best of both the bar and the kitchen.

70. TIPPECANOE PLACE

620 West Washington, South Bend, IN 46601
(219) 234-9077
Open Monday-Friday for lunch & dinner;
dinner only on Saturday; Sunday Brunch.

This elegant mansion, the original home built by
the Studebaker family in 1888, is the embodiment of
everything great wealth could suggest in the 1880's.
Its 4 levels of exquisite architecture and detailing,
including 40 rooms and 20 fireplaces, provided a
magnificent backdrop for many lavish parties,
weddings and balls that were prized invitations by
South Bend society. Today, Tippecanoe Place is still
known for its hospitality and as a gracious setting
for fine dining. With the exception of a modern
kitchen and bar being added, great attention has
been paid to preserving the original atmosphere of
these grand rooms that are now the dining areas. Its
award-winning fare includes a wonderful variety of
appetizers, entrees, and desserts created daily by
their pastry chef. The house specialty is "perfect"
prime rib. Sunday Brunch is a veritable feast,
offering a wide variety of appealing selections.
Reservations are recommended.

71. OAKWOOD INN

849 East Lake View Road, Syracuse, IN 46567
(Hidden entrance, 1 1/2 blocks off Highway 13)
(219) 457-5600
Open Tuesday-Saturday for breakfast, lunch
& dinner; breakfast & brunch on Sunday;
closed Monday. (Continental breakfast in winter.)

Escape to this retreat center owned by the Oakwood
Foundation for Adult Christian Ministeries, Inc.
Located on 40 acres on Lake Wawasee, the largest
natural lake in northern Indiana, the beautifully
appointed oak structure that houses the hotel/
restaurant and surrounding grounds are designed
to provide an environment for peaceful reflection.
Enjoy dining in a relaxed setting with a wall of
windows overlooking the lake. A full service,
moderately priced menu, specializing in fresh fish,
prime rib, steak, pasta and stir fry, is complement-
ed by wonderful pastries prepared by the chef on
premises. Weekend buffets feature fish and seafood
on Friday and prime rib on Saturday. (Smoke-free
environment; no alcohol served.)

72. STRONGBOW TURKEY INN

Junction of S.R. 49 & U.S. 30, Valparaiso, IN 46383
(219) 462-5121; (800) 462-5121
Open daily for lunch & dinner.

Now in its 3rd generation of family ownership, the
restaurant was named after the Potowatomi Indian
chief who lived on the land with his tribe in the 19th
century. The grandparents of the present owners
began raising their first crop of turkeys in 1937. In
1940, both U.S. Highway 30 and the Inn opened
simultanously with a 28-seat dining room, 8 cabins
for overnight guests and 3 gas pumps. It has steadi-
ly grown over the years into the complex it is today
with public and private dining rooms, a cocktail
lounge, bakery and retail outlet, plus a premier
banquet and convention center accommodating up

to 500 guests. Strongbow offers sandwiches and
salads for lunch and beef and seafood selections for
dinner, but obviously turkey dishes are their
signature items, including the traditional turkey
dinner, famous turkey pie, and adaptations of other
dishes, such as turkey schnitzel and turkey oskar.
"One of the finest examples of Hoosier hospitality
and fine dining."

73. BARBEE INN
HOTEL BAR & GRILL

3620 North Barbee, Warsaw, IN 46580
(219) 834-2984
Open daily for dinner only.

Located in the North Webster area between Big
Barbee and Little Barbee Lakes, this late 19th
century hotel has been beautifully renovated
and offers plenty of rustic charm. You will find
whatever you have a taste for on the casual,
"upscale" menu, from the traditional steaks, chops,
chicken, ribs and pastas to excellent veal, lamb,
seafood and duck selections. No fast food served
here—your dinner will be prepared after you place
your order.

74. MOSAIQUE

115 South Buffalo Street
Warsaw, IN 46580
(219) 269-5080
Open daily for dinner
only; closed Sunday.

With the desire to bring
"big city" dining to
Warsaw, award-winning
chefs Nancy Sideris & Alexis Sideris purchased this
130-year old dime-store turned furniture store and
redesigned the 3 floors to create an architecturally
unique restaurant. The name originates from the
specially commissioned mosaic-tile glass bar high-
lighting the interior. The atmosphere is that of a
studio with Impressionist art and fresh flowers
decorating the nooks and crannies. You will notice
an ethnic influence in the American/California
cuisine, reflecting the freshest available indigenous
ingredients: vegetables, herbs, Maple Leaf Farm
duck and Doc Miller striped bass, to name just a
few. Additional items on the menu include steak,
lamb and veal entrees.

Southern Indiana

75. THE SHERMAN HOUSE

35 South Main Street, Batesville, IN 47006
(812) 934-2407; (800) 445-4939
Open daily for breakfast, lunch & dinner.

This popular inn has served as a landmark in the area since it opened in 1852. Decorated with pictures of General Sherman and renderings of art from the Civil War period, you can relax and unwind in the old-world atmosphere and enjoy some of the tastiest food in southern Indiana. The specialty is traditional German fare—weinerschnitzel, bratwurst and sauerbraten—but features wonderful American dishes as well.

76. INN AT BETHLEHEM

101 Walnut Street, Bethlehem, IN 47104
(812) 293-3975
By Reservation Only: Dinner Thursday-Saturday; Sunday Brunch July thru September; lunch for parties of 8 or more.

This 1830 federal-style manor resting on 26 acres is listed in the National Register of Historic Landmarks. Located in the remote river valley between Jeffersonville and Madison, the Inn is tucked away in a very beautiful and serene setting overlooking the Ohio River and the hills of Kentucky. The Inn and Lodge are furnished with many period antiques and all 10 rooms have private baths. Many different weekend and special occasion packages are available. Meals are graciously served in a beautiful setting, featuring New American cuisine prepared by the chef with over 10 years of experience. This quiet retreat is the perfect getaway! Call for reservations.

77. THE IRISH LION®

212 West 5th (Kirkwood), Bloomington, IN 47404
(812) 336-9076
Open Monday-Saturday for lunch & dinner until "the wee hours"; Sunday for dinner until midnight.

This long, narrow tavern has been serving food and drink since 1882--the ice house out back, turn-of-the-century metal ceiling, and the many antiques decorating the interior are all reminders of its earlier days. In Ireland, where no one point is more than 70 miles from the sea, a lot of seafood is consumed. Thus, after the customary drink to begin the meal, appetizers of shrimp, crabheachain, oysters Rockefeller (an original recipe), or Blarney puff balls are offered. When you're ready for the main course, choose the corned beef & cabbage, Irish stew, leg of lamb or chops, prime rib, live lobster, shrimp, or perhaps the "rineanna"--duckling half with apple-fennel bread stuffing. Then, top off your meal with a piece of apple walnut cake or whiskey pie! Irish soda bread is baked on site.

78. UPTOWN CAFE

102 East Kirkwood, Bloomington, IN 47408
(812) 339-0900
Open Monday-Saturday for breakfast, lunch & dinner; Sunday brunch.

A popular spot for breakfast when it first opened, the Uptown moved to a larger location and is now a full service restaurant. Located just off the downtown square, it attracts a broad cross section of people in this busy college town. The bistro-style cafe features "new American eclectic cuisine", which means a variety of cooking styles--Cajun, Mediterranean and Classical French--using a variety of different ingredients. Everything is made from scratch, using the freshest local and regional produce, plus fresh fish and Black Angus steaks. Unusual but tasty soups include West African peanut, Oyster Artichoke, and Mulligatawny.

79. DILEGGE'S

607 North Main, Evansville, IN 47711
(812) 428-3004
Open Monday-Friday for lunch & dinner; dinner only on Saturday; closed Sunday.

With ancestors from Italy, this family-owned restaurant guarantees superb Italian cuisine, specializing in all homemade sauces and desserts. The menu also includes a nice selection of chicken, beef, seafood, veal and pasta dishes. Surrounded by many beautiful plants and photos of flowers, you will enjoy dining in this casual, relaxed atmosphere.

80. DOGTOWN TAVERN

6201 Old Henderson Road, Evansville, IN 47712
(812) 423-0808
Open Monday-Saturday for lunch & dinner;
closed Sunday.

The Dogtown Tavern got its name over 100 years ago from hunters leaving their dogs tied up outside while they indulged in the best fried catfish (fiddlers) in the world. You can get there by boat or car. It's off the beaten path, not much to look at, but a lot of fun and good food with a real flavor of the good old boys.

81. HILLTOP INN

1100 Harmony Way, Evansville, IN 47720
(812) 422-1757
Open Monday-Saturday for lunch & dinner;
closed Sunday.

Built in 1839, this restaurant was originally an old saloon and stage coach stop. Located high on a hill just 2 miles from the Ohio River, it was a popular stop for weary travelers. It has maintained a very rustic, country atmosphere and features a 75-100 year old back bar. Hilltop offers your basic down home country cookin'—fried chicken, steaks and fiddlers—but if you're the more adventuresome type, you must try the brain sandwich, an unusual but popular menu item!

82. WOLF'S BAR-B-QUE

1414 East Columbia Street, Evansville, IN 47711
(812) 423-3599
Open daily for lunch & dinner.

Now owned by the third generation of Wolfs, their barbecue has been recognized as one of the top 100 foods in the U.S. and has been served to over two million people in the past 10 years, including well-known celebrities and politicians. The first restaurant in Indiana to have curb service and a drive-up window, it now seats 360 in the main dining room and has become an Evansville family tradition.

83. YWCA TEA ROOM

118 Vine Street, Evansville, IN 47708
(812) 422-1191
Open Monday-Friday for lunch only.

Founded in 1911, the YWCA provided housing, recreation and hot meals to the women staying in the original old white house; the current YWCA was constructed on the same spot in 1925. The Tea Room grew in popularity when they changed from serving plate lunches to a wider selection of soups, salads, sandwiches and desserts and offered free meeting rooms to groups who came for lunch. The dining room offers a warm and pleasant setting, decorated with pink geraniums that bloom all year. The staff and board of directors create the recipes, including the popular herb-dill chicken salad. Other tasty items include the veggie melt, pumpkin bread, and fruit and tuna salad made with apples, raisins and walnuts. Dessert specialties include French silk and pecan pie.

84. CHATEAU POMIJE

25060 Jacobs Road, Guilford, IN 47022
(800) 791-9463
Open Wednesday-Sunday for dinner;
Friday-Sunday for lunch; closed Monday
and Tuesday.

Chateau Pomije is nestled on 100 acres amid some of Indiana's most picturesque scenery. It combines the captivating atmosphere of a fully working winery with the charm, elegance and character of the restaurant itself—a reconstructed 100-year-old timbered barn featuring a dramatic stone fireplace, the largest of its kind in Indiana. Begin with a tour of the winery and sample some of their award-winning wines. Then sit down to a wonderful selection of homemade favorites: generous cuts of mouth-watering steak aged to perfection, delicious pork tenderloin, and Indiana's most famous BBQ ribs and chicken, served with plenty of fresh vegetables, homegrown salads & bread. No one leaves hungry!

85. HAUB'S STEAK HOUSE

Corner of Main & Haub, Haubstadt, IN 47639
(812) 768-6462; (800) 654-1158
Open Monday-Saturday for dinner only.

This former warehouse built in the early 1900's has been remodeled into a charming southern colonial straight out of Williamsburg. Decorated with wood paneling and large chandeliers, each dining room carries out the colonial theme...dine in the Manor Room or the Kensington Room. There are over 50 entrees on the menu to choose from, including prime beef and fresh seafood. Reservations are recommended on weekends.

86. LOG INN

Off I-64 on Warrenton Road, Haubstadt, IN 47639
(812) 867-3216
Open Tuesday-Saturday for dinner only;
closed Sunday and Monday.

Built in 1825 as one of the main noon day stage coach stops and trading posts between Evansville and Vincennes, this historic building is officially recognized as the oldest restaurant in Indiana and the oldest original log inn. The full cellar beneath the inn was also an underground railroad stop during the Civil War. Surrounded by many antiques, including the main bar, back bar and cash register purchased in 1892 and an old 1910 nickelodeon, you can dine on their specialty of fried chicken and family style dinners. Ask to be seated in the same original log room that Abraham Lincoln visited in November, 1844!

87. NISBET INN
6701 Nisbet Rd. (I-64, Exit 18), Haubstadt, IN 47639
(812) 963-9305
Open Tuesday-Saturday for lunch & dinner.

Located at the site of an old railroad crossing about 10 miles north of Evansville, the Inn was built in 1912 to serve the rail traveler as an oasis for food, drink and lodging. Even though a train hasn't passed through since 1971, the architecture has remained true to its original design and it is still a popular place for food and drink. You will enjoy an atmosphere of warmth and hospitality where you can easily imagine yourself in an earlier and more relaxed time. Its reputation draws patrons from all over to sample some of the best barbecue around, along with a variety of sandwiches, homemade soups and pies. A nice selection of beer, wine and cocktails is available.

88. MEZZALUNA RESTAURANT
104 North Water Street, Henderson, KY 42420
(502) 826-9401
Open Monday-Saturday for lunch; dinner on Friday only.

Mezzaluna means "crescent moon" in Italian and the restaurant draws from its Italian heritage by displaying a picture of the owner's dad as "the man in the moon." A small, late 19th century house with an outside patio, view of the river and an active herb and flower garden provides a picturesque setting for this "artsy cafe." Pine floors, a painted rug, and dark green, cardinal, khaki and black furnishings add to the casual atmosphere. The walls provide a gallery for the work of area artists. The lunch menu features deli-style food ordered at the counter and delivered to your table, including 10 different sandwiches, tossed green, vegetable, fruit and pasta salads, plus daily "white plate specials" such as eggplant lasagna, grilled portabello sandwiches and rosemary chicken pot pie. The Friday night dinner menu, which changes weekly with the same item seldom repeated, features foods "with a twist on the traditional", particularly upscale pastas and trendy foods that you would find in New York City restaurants.

89. SCHNITZELBANK RESTAURANT

393 Third Avenue, Jasper, IN 47546
(812) 482-2640
Open Monday-Saturday for breakfast, lunch and dinner; closed Sunday.

This large, alpine-looking German restaurant, complete with a working Glockenspiel out front, is located on the original site of a small local tavern called Schnitzelbank, the name of a bench that woodcrafters whittle on. Outstanding German food is served by waitresses dressed in drindl skirts; the colorful murals on the walls of the dining rooms will transport you to the mountains of Germany! Weinerschnitzel and beef rolladen are house favorites, but steak, prime rib and hand-breaded shrimp are also available. The salad bar features 50 different items, including ribble (round Geman noodles) and turnip kraut. Sample one of the 100 different imported beers or order your favorite American brand.

90. WHISKY'S
334 Front Street, Lawrenceburg, IN 47025
(812) 537-4239
Open Monday-Friday for lunch & dinner; dinner only on Saturday; closed Sunday.

Old Lawrenceburg (Newtown) is the home of Seagram's Distillery and the restaurant is named for its location in the "whiskey city" ! Two buildings, one dating from 1850 and the other rumored to have been a button factory in 1835, are joined by an atrium and feature five dining areas: a formal dining room, the enclosed courtyard with an outdoorsy feeling, the Malt Room, the Seagram's Room with a huge metal cut-out of a Seagram's bottle on the ceiling, and the cozy backroom bar. The overall atmosphere is dark and quiet with candles and fresh flowers on the tables. The atrium is decorated with a collection of birdhouses, and a post office from an old grocery store provides unique seating for 4. The item most in demand is the barbecued ribs, smoked with a secret sauce, but the Dealer's choice of steaks and smoked chicken are other popular selections. Sandwiches (try the Lawrence-burger "your way") and daily lunch specials are also available.

91. THE OVERLOOK
3 Miles S of I-64, Exit 92, Leavenworth, IN 47137
(812) 739-4264
Open daily for breakfast, lunch & dinner; closed Christmas Day.

Overlooking a sweeping panorama of forested hills and the Ohio River as it arches around a horseshoe bend, you will enjoy magnificent views from every window in this appropriately-named restaurant.

The Overlook has earned a reputation over the years for good home cooking at very reasonable prices, offered in a warm and casual setting. Specialties include their popular creamed chicken served over homemade biscuits and a terrific beef manhattan, plus country fried chicken, ham, pork chops and seafood are additional selections. A nice variety of sandwiches is also available.

92. STOLL'S COUNTRY INN
State Road 54 West, Linton, IN 47441
(812) 847-2477
Open Monday-Saturday for breakfast, lunch & dinner.

Enjoy country dining with an Amish influence, in both the decor and the cooking. Everything is homemade and served buffet style, including country fried chicken, steaks, and real mashed potatoes. Chicken and dumplings is a house specialty. Breakfast items include grits, fried mush, country ham, homemade sausage, and their very special creamed rice. (No alcohol served.)

93. UPPER CRUST
209 West Main Street, Madison, IN 47250
(812) 265-6727
Open Tuesday-Saturday for dinner.

The Upper Crust is the creme de la creme of Madison dining. This small, graciously intimate restaurant with a European ambience, complete with white tablecloths, candlelight and classical background music, provides the perfect backdrop for a superb meal. Chef Nick Izamis brings a continental flair to a wonderful selection of entrees, cooked to order, including dishes with Greek, Italian, French and Southwestern influences. Reservations are required on Fridays & Saturdays.

94. MILAN RAILROAD INN

Main & Carr Streets, Milan, IN 47031
(812) 654-2800; (800) 448-7405
Open daily for lunch & dinner.

Built in 1915 as the Keonig Hotel, the restaurant is situated next to the railroad tracks and at least 6 to 8 trains pass through every day! For avid train fans, a front porch with 3 booths provides an excellent viewing area while enjoying your meal. Along with train memorabilia and old tools, the restaurant is also decorated with information about the town's memorable 1954 state championship basketball team featured in the movie "Hoosiers". The unique soup and salad bar features 18 different dishes, including bread pudding with rum sauce, and "everything is homemade except the cottage cheese." They are best known for great fried chicken, but pork chops, steaks, ham steak and Angus prime rib are also popular.

95. NASHVILLE HOUSE

Main & VanBuren Streets, Nashville, IN 47448
(812) 988-4554
Open for lunch & dinner daily; closed Tuesdays.

An Indiana restaurant guide would not be complete without mentioning the Nashville House and their famous fried biscuits with homemade apple butter! Originally the site of a hotel built in 1859, that structure burned down in 1944 and was rebuilt in 1947 as a restaurant and country store. Native Brown County poplar and oak timbers and floors, red and white checked tablecloths, and a wonderful collection of antiques decorate the interior. In fact, the owner has been approached to sell his antiques but he refuses, saying he wouldn't have anything else to hang on the walls! Sandwiches are served on wonderful homemade bread for lunch; country fried chicken, ham and turkey dinners are available all day. Special homemade desserts include the famous pecan nut pie, cobblers and cream pies.

96. RED GERANIUM

504 North Street, New Harmony, IN 47631
(812) 682-4431
Open Tuesday-Sunday for lunch & dinner; closed Monday. (Closed for lunch January-March.)

This award-winning restaurant is located next to the New Harmony Inn in this historic community, the site where two of the earliest communal societies settled in Indiana. Filled with a warm and gracious 19th century atmosphere, you will enjoy gourmet dining in a relaxed setting before or after a tour of the town. The Garden Room with its painted orchard ceiling provides an intimate setting for small dinner parties. The menu features many regional as well as continental favorites, including their famous spinach salad with house dressing, warm homemade bread, char prime steak, and irresistible Shaker lemon pie. Red Geranium Cellars offer the connoisseur a wide selection of fine wines served at your table or at the Grapevine Bar.

97. JOE HUBER'S FAMILY FARM, ORCHARD & RESTAURANT

2421 Scottsville Road, Starlight, IN 47106
(812) 923-5255
Open daily for lunch & dinner;
closed December 23 through February.

Started in 1967 as a roadside fruit and vegetable market, it soon became a place where you could pick your own produce. The regular customers often commented that they would like something to eat, so in 1983 a restaurant was built adjacent to the market. As you enter this country restaurant, now seating 400, you are greeted by family portraits and a huge painting of the Huber farm covering one wall. You can also dine outdoors on the awning covered patio in the summer, surrounded by beautiful flower, fruit and vegetable gardens. Seasonal produce from the Huber and surrounding farms accompany the main course selections of country-fried chicken or Huber honey ham. Homemade dumplings and deep fried biscuits are also tasty additions. Tempting desserts include fresh strawberry pie (in season), homemade peach cobbler, and coconut or peanut butter cream pies.